Using th
with Children

Rosemary Cox

GROVE BOOKS LIMITED
RIDLEY HALL RD CAMBRIDGE CB3 9HU

Contents

At the end of each chapter there are questions for further reflection,
which can be used individually or as the basis of group discussion.

To the children whom I have taught
And who have taught me
And to the friends who have prayed and supported me
Through this project
Especially John:
Thank you.

The Cover Illustration is by Peter Ashton

First Impression March 2000
ISSN 1365-490X
ISBN 1 85174 428 2

1
Introduction

It is Saturday night. Sunday morning looms, and with it the privilege and responsibility of leading a bright-eyed group of self-styled 'Young Disciples.' We meet in the village hall opposite the church, joining the adult congregation towards the end of the communion service, going up for a blessing or the bread and wine. The youngest of the children is five, the oldest thirteen. In this rural parish we are a new group, and do not yet have sufficient leaders to allow us to form two groups. But we work well together, the children and I and the other helpers, growing with and learning from one another. Some of the children are from 'church' families, some are not. Two of the children (nine-year olds) had been coming to church on their own for several months before the group began, sitting through *Book of Common Prayer* services in a chilly country church, younger by about fifty years than the rest of the congregation. In fact the group was eventually started as a direct result of prayer and a sense of God's calling, after two young teenagers spontaneously came to a family service one Sunday morning, having heard the church bells ringing, but never having attended a church service before. They returned the following week with three younger sisters, and I held an impromptu meeting for them on the lawn outside the church—there being nowhere else available at the time. Over the next two months we planned a children's and young people's group, working out our priorities. We would have fun and get to know each other, and we would pray, worship, and study the Bible together. But how should we study the Bible? What could we expect from the children? How would our activities in the group be related to what the rest of the church was doing?

One of my particular concerns over the years has arisen from noticing that comparatively little thought has been given to the underlying principles governing the ways in which we use the Bible in children's work. My experience is that, in churches generally, our grasp of the issues involved in using the Bible with *adults* is poor. How much more limited is our understanding of the ways in which it might be appropriate to use the Bible with *children*?

It is true that there are on the Christian market various resources for those teaching children on Sundays, often in the form of curricula covering a term or more's worth of teaching. Many of these materials are carefully thought through and well presented, and could provide children with some good biblical foundations if used consistently and wisely. Nevertheless, I am left with the nagging suspicion—no doubt borne of my own experience—that the temptation for the harassed (and often untrained) children's group leader is to pick a lesson, or series of lessons, off the teaching manual 'shelf' and then present it more or less as given, with little personal understanding of how the week's study passage might fit into the scheme of the Bible as a whole, or of how it might appropriately be interpreted. This sort of approach inevitably leaves children with a disjointed impression of the biblical witness, and offers them no understanding either of the recurring theological themes of the Bible, or of how such themes might apply to them. I have noticed, too, that some teaching materials tend to focus on narrative, at the expense of other forms of biblical literature. No doubt this may partially reflect the fact that children (and their teachers?) are typically comfortable with the story form. ('Tell me another story.' 'Well, once upon a time…') The whole biblical counsel, though, comes to us in a variety of genres, some of which, I suggest, children are well able to engage with. Children have their own experiences of dreams, poetry-making, and letter-writing, of the challenging of perceived injustices ('That's not fair!') and the bringing of good news. Given appropriate guidelines as to methods of interpretation, there is no reason why they should not be introduced to more than just biblical stories. Moreover, in much of the teaching materials I have examined there is an expectation that the teacher will give the 'point' of the lesson, the interpretation of the passage. It is rarely the case, it seems to me, that the children themselves are seen as interpreters, with valid perspectives on the biblical text which we have never dreamed of. Yet we know that children *are* interpreters from the moment they are born, constantly attempting to make sense of the data around them. It seems to me appropriate, therefore, that in our use of the Bible with children we begin to help them in the interpretive process, teaching them how to ask appropriate questions of the text, working out with them appropriate applications.

My interest, therefore, is in examining the issues *underlying* our approach to using the Bible with children. Before we ask the practical 'how' questions, (which I shall also want to address here) I think we have to ask the 'why' questions which logically precede them.[1] If we examine the underlying principles involved, we shall be enabled to apply our insights to our teaching in a variety of contexts in appropriate ways.

For Further Reflection

In receiving teaching from Scripture, on what occasions have you been told 'the point' and on what occasions have you been enabled to discover the point for yourself? Which have proved the most enduring learning experiences?

---

1   This is the approach of R and G Gobbel in their seminal work in this area *The Bible: A Child's Playground* (London: SCM, 1986).

2

What is the Bible?

In thinking about using the Bible with children, it seems logical first to consider what our understanding of the Bible is, and then to ask what our understanding of children is. Just as a good host at a party knows something about the guests he introduces to each other, so we, as we introduce the Bible and children to each other, need an awareness of the nature of each.

So far as the Bible is concerned, one writer has said:

> 'The present position of the Bible in the Christian churches has been well put in a single sentence: "We thought we were agreed upon the Bible until we opened it." This uncertainty about what the Bible is and what it is for does not make guidance about its use with children any easier.'[2]

Obviously there are various models for the ways in which we may understand Scripture, but in children's ministry there seems to have been little overt examination of the ways in which we choose our models. In consequence, inadequate or inappropriate models are used. Too often, it seems to me, the impression is given simply of the Bible as somehow a 'special book,' or as a series of apparently unrelated books, which is in some undefined way supposed to carry authority for us. Given the general lack of practical and theological training for most children's group teachers, it is understandable that the teachers themselves might find it difficult to move beyond these models. The burden, therefore, is on those with some theological experience to explore and articulate more appropriate paradigms.

What Paradigms of the Bible Do We Have?

First of all, I would make an obvious but important point. The Bible is not actually a children's book. It was written by adults for adults. In Deuteronomy, a clear mandate is given to the Israelite community to 'memorize (God's) laws and tell them to your children over and over again' (Deuteronomy 6.6, 7 from the *Contemporary English Version*). The onus, however, is clearly on the adults to pass on the commandments. How much more must this be the case where the overall biblical content is concerned.

Clearly, for children as well as for adults, the Bible is not just a collection of stories. Neither is it a 'rule book' for Christian living, simply prescriptive and immediately applicable to all the situations in which twenty-first-century

---

2   John Gray, *What About the Children?* (London: SCM, 1970) p 39.

people find themselves.

Nor is it even a presentation of a logical system of thought. Paul Tournier, coming to the Bible as a doctor and asking what bearing it might have on the problems of life which confronted him, found that, just as the Bible reflects the breadth of human experience, so it is full of paradox.[3] It is precisely this richness of the Bible which defies easy attempts to describe or define it.

The Bible contains no neat formulae—or if it does, they still need to be interpreted. Scripture itself is variously portrayed as 'God's word' (Ps 119.9), 'light for the path' (Ps 119.105), 'God-breathed, useful for teaching, rebuking, correcting and training in righteousness' (2 Tim 3.16)—and as an object of study which, apart from a relationship with Christ, will not actually prove life-giving (John 5.39, 40). If Bible teachers wish to teach by topics (for instance, 'What is God like?,' 'What are people like?,' 'Suffering,' 'Evil') the task of drawing out the biblical counsel is not easy, and immediately involves a hermeneutical exercise, whether this is explicitly acknowledged or not.

A Variety of Paradigms?

Traditionally, theologians have applied powerful concepts such as 'authority' and 'revelation' when speaking of the biblical witness, but in recent years scholarship, both liberal and evangelical, has begun to question whether, in fact, it is right to apply only *one* model of understanding to the whole of the canon. The Bible contains many different types of literature, and the different types call for different ways both of understanding and of responding. So, it is argued, the summary of the law, with its call for unequivocal obedience, could properly be called 'authoritative,' but The Song of Songs, with its account of the feelings and sensations of one pair of lovers at one particular time, could not.[4] The very concept of 'authority' is arguably quite a 'male' one, drawn from the world of power-relations, and we need to value, as well, more feminine ways of understanding the effect the Bible is to have on our lives—perhaps using words such as influence, encouragement, and inspiration.[5] Maybe, too, children—traditionally powerless and dependent— might want to suggest models for Scripture of their own, if only they were able to articulate them: the Word as 'fighter' for them,[6] perhaps, or as nurturer.[7]

---

3   Paul Tournier, *A Doctor's Casebook* (London: SCM, 1954) pp 19, 20.
4   On this question in post-modern context see Richard Bauckham *Scripture and Authority Today* Grove Biblical booklet B 12.
5   See D Clines, *The Bible and the Modern World* (Sheffield: Sheffield Academic Press,1997) pp 90–91.
6   As in Ephesians 6.17: 'the sword of the Spirit.'
7   See Hebrews 5.12: God's word as 'milk' and 'solid food.'

A 'Shaper' of Character?

This rethinking of the model or models we use to apply to Scripture has obvious implications for those of us who teach, because it forces us to ask 'What are we trying to *do* when we introduce people to the Bible? In what way are we saying the biblical text should carry meaning for our lives?' A model I find helpful when thinking of using the Bible with children is that of the Bible as a 'shaper' of our character—that is, a shaper of that mix of ideas, beliefs and ways of behaving which goes to make up who we are. I am becoming increasingly convinced that the Bible contains less direct teaching material than we sometimes think. There is the law, and there are the epistles, but there is also a great deal of material which influences us indirectly, such as stories, images, and parables, which affect us subliminally and help to form our values.[8] I want to suggest two ways in which it might be helpful to think of the Bible as a 'shaper' in our work with children. Firstly, the Bible tells us the 'Big Story' of God, his community, and our place in that community. Secondly, within the frame of this Big Story, the Bible shapes us by providing us with a variety of types of teaching material, set in different literary forms, with differing teaching goals. If we are to nurture children in the faith, we will need to understand this diversity of forms for ourselves, learning how to interpret appropriately, and teaching children to do the same.

We will look at each of these—the 'Big Story' and the diversity of forms—in turn.

For Further Reflection

Which parts of Scripture have had the most impact on the way you think about the world and yourself, and the way you live your life?

Which parts of Scripture do you turn to in a crisis, and why?

If you had to describe to a non-Christian friend what the Bible is in one sentence, what would you say?

---

8   See J Goldingay, *Approaches to Old Testament Interpretation* (Leicester: Apollos, 1990) pp 41–43.

3

'The Big Story'

'The story form is a cultural universal; everyone everywhere enjoys stories. The story, then, is not just some casual entertainment; it reflects a basic and powerful form in which we make sense of the world and experience. Indeed, some people claim that the story form reflects a fundamental structure of our minds...Telling a story is a way of establishing meaning.'[9]

Sunday School-type teaching has typically focussed on an individual story, usually with a particular character at its centre, without setting the story in its overall theological context. The weakness of this approach is that it can both lead to a disjointed understanding and actually be misleading. Individual stories, or collections of stories (particularly from the Old Testament) can, if taken at face value, leave impressions of God and his call to us which are far from whole and still further from 'good news.' The stories of the Judges, beloved of some primary curricula for their colour and drama, provide a good example. Samson, held up for his boldness and strength, was mostly thuggish and sexually unrestrained, and his sadistic treatment of foxes alone (firelighters for Philistine cornfields) would have merited a prison sentence today. Jephtha, and his determination to kill his daughter as a result of a foolish vow, is the stuff of video horror. Even when individual stories (such as those from the life of Jesus) carry a less 'mixed' message, they can still seem disconnected. The link between Old and New Testaments perhaps never becomes clear, nor may there be an answer to the question 'But what has this got to do with *me*—here and now, in my playground, classroom, home?'

The corrective, it seems to me, is to regularly 'tell the whole story' of the people of God, not only to adults, but to children. Telling the 'big story,' I believe, not only helps to make sense of the Bible, and accords with learning theories about how we make meaning by making connections. It also allows children to find their own place in the story. And it is an approach which is rooted in biblical tradition. 'What do these stones mean?' ask the children of Israel, long after the crossing of the River Jordan. To which the elders reply with the story of their deliverance from the Egyptians (Joshua 4.6, 7). The telling of the story not only served to consolidate the community, uniting its members in a common history. It also gave an opportunity for the younger

---

9 Kieran Egan, *Teaching as Storytelling* (London: Routledge, 1988) pp 2, 37.

ones, who had not experienced the original events, to identify with the community, appropriating the story for themselves as it was told and retold by their parents and grandparents. The story ritual is still played out time and again in the Jewish community, at festivals such as Passover, and at the Friday night *seders*. As Christians, this is an aspect of our common life that we should perhaps recover—making the most of our 'highlight' festivals such as Christmas and Easter, and celebrating at 'thanksgiving meals,' not only in church but at home, round the table, with family and friends.

So What Story Shall We Tell Our Children?

In *The New Testament and the People of God,* N T Wright suggests seeing the biblical story as a drama in five 'acts.' Creation constitutes the first act; the fall the second; the exile the third; and the life, death and resurrection of Jesus the fourth. The fifth act begins with the inauguration of the church by the Holy Spirit, but it is not finished. We, the people of God in our time, are characters in the fifth act, and have a role to play in determining how the drama will unfold.[10] In other words, we are part of the 'big story.' And this means that we, and our children, will have to so identify with and be able to interpret the story, that we will be able, creatively and appropriately, to develop it. 'Being true to that liberating, innovative feature of biblical tradition means not photocopying what Jesus and the first disciples said and did, but pushing forward in the direction they point.'[11] I see a double challenge for us, as teachers, in this. We need both to tell children the story, and to give them the tools with which to begin to interpret it.

I like Wright's model for understanding the biblical story, and feel that it can be especially useful in work with children. It affirms each person's value and role in the community of the people of God, and can therefore be a helpful corrective to the common 'invisibility' and lack of voice of children in the church at present. It also draws on the qualities of creativity, imagination and adventurousness which typify children, and which will be needed if they are to see themselves as characters in the unfolding story. The model also offers a doorway into the area of interpretation, offering possibilities of applying the insights of the biblical communities in our own communities in appropriate ways. As the initial quotation from Egan suggests, the 'big story' approach also works well as a teaching tool, and is perhaps naturally reflective of the way our minds seek to make sense of things. Moreover, for children, the approach not only allows them to find themselves in the story, but allows them to grow with it. Adopting Wright's model may well challenge our notions of whether or not children really are part of the people of

---

10 N T Wright, *The New Testament and the People of God* (London: SPCK, 1992) pp 141, 142.
11 Brian Wren, *What Language Shall I Borrow?* (London: SCM, 1989) p 133.

God now (as opposed to 'the church of tomorrow'), and whether or not they too can be inspired by the Spirit to interpret and develop the teachings of Jesus in the way he wants. And we may find that if we enable children to take their place alongside us as members of the living, growing, body of Christ, with something to give as well as to receive, we, as much as they, will be enriched.

For Further Reflection

How clearly do you think you have grasped the 'Big Story' of the Bible? Could you explain it simply to another, or are you still struggling yourself?

What has helped you most in developing an overview of Scripture? What difference has having an overview made to your reading of individual passages?

How have you dealt with difficulties (such as those mentioned in connexion with the story of Samson) in either Old or New Testament passages—for yourself or for others?

4
Different Types of Literature

While it is important to give children an overview of the Bible, we must also teach children to handle correctly the different parts of Scripture. We have already noted that there has been an emphasis in children's ministry on teaching the narratives at the expense of other forms of literature. And in my experience these narratives are not always handled appropriately. Bible characters are seldom examples to follow, and Bible stories should rarely be taken as laying down doctrine.

The mistake, I think, has been in the failure to incorporate the insights of biblical criticism into our work with children. While there has been, in recent years, a sensitivity to questions of *historical* context in children's teaching materials, issues of *literary* context, including, in particular, sensitivity to different types of genre, have largely been ignored. (The problem is exacerbated by the fact that the children's group teachers—generally untrained and unsupported—often have little understanding of these issues themselves. Moreover they have usually received little or no encouragement to do some of the basic theological study which is considered essential where the work of teaching adults is concerned).

Different Genres

The Bible comes to us in a variety of forms, and each form has a different authorial intent and purpose. Each must therefore be understood on its own terms, with different sorts of questions to be asked of it. There are stories, poetry, parables, dreams, visions, letters, and wisdom material, to name just some. Many people, though, teach as though this variety did not exist, understanding and presenting the whole content in the same, often rather literal, way. We need, rather, to teach children, and adults, to handle the biblical material with an understanding of what the text is actually trying to *do*, encouraging them to ask appropriate questions of it, make connections between the biblical world and their own, and apply the insights of the text to their lives.[12]

Although genre analysis is a specialized discipline, its understanding of the different forms of literature can, I think, be fairly easily appropriated and applied by those who use the Bible with children. There are numerous ways of classifying the various genres, but McCartney and Clayton suggest

---

12 See Jean Holm, 'What Shall We Tell The Children?' *Theology* vol 76 (1973) pp 141–148.

the following, fairly straightforward, list: theological history;[13] law; poetry; prophecy; parables; epistles; and apocalyptic.[14] To this list I would possibly add wisdom material as a separate category.

Different Teaching Styles

In *The Creative Word*,[15] Walter Brueggemann points to the way in which the Old Testament contains not only different forms of literature, but different ways of instructing. In Jeremiah 18.18, the conspirators plotting against the prophet say:

> 'Come, let's make plans against Jeremiah; for the teaching of the law by the priest will not be lost, nor will counsel from the wise, nor the word from the prophets. So come, let's attack him with our tongues and pay no attention to anything he says.'

Brueggemann argues that this summons to conspiracy contains a summary of Israelite belief: the law (Torah) of the priest; the counsel of the wise; and the word of the prophets. There were three authoritative offices, or agents of instruction (Priest, Wise, Prophet), and three sources of knowledge (Torah, counsel, word). The three forms of knowledge were contained in distinct bodies of biblical material, which each had its own way of teaching and influencing the Israelite community. The Torah was 'core' material. It was to be communicated as *given*, and it was what identified and held together the body of orthodox believers. The prophetic material (in which Brueggemann includes the historical books) had to be heard as a *challenge* to the establishment in its misuse of what had been given, and its misplaced satisfaction with the *status quo*. The wisdom material, dealing with the day-to-day stuff of life in community, required not so much an acceptance of the given, or a reception of challenge, as a 'teasing out' of the practicalities of faith in the everyday circumstances of life. As one moved from Torah, to the prophets, to the wisdom literature, the teaching style became less didactic, and the learner took more initiative. In response to all the material, an obedience was required, but the *way* of obedience differed according to the type of instruction.

I think there is something we can learn here about the different ways in which it may be appropriate to teach, depending on the type of material we are dealing with. While, for instance, the law (do not steal; do not covet) can be communicated unequivocally, the prophetic material will require more

---

13 This shows how God has acted in the past in relation to his people, and how he has created a
    community which should now obey and trust him.
14 D McCartney and C Clayton, *Let the Reader Understand* (Wheaton: Bridgepoint 1994) pp 210–228.
15 (Philadelphia: Fortress, 1988).

engagement from the learner. We have to help children ask, for instance, 'Where is injustice?' 'What is idolatry?' 'What does God want us to do about it?' The wisdom literature, in the Old Testament, and the epistles in the New, require even more engagement. We have to help children begin to ask, in the knotty and troubling daily details (which were mostly never foreseen by the biblical authors), 'What does a holy God require of me here?' Or, as the letters 'WWJD,' on the children's multicoloured wristbands, remind them to ask: 'What would Jesus do?' In helping children to grow in the faith, we not only have to teach them what we know; we must encourage them to develop a biblically-based wisdom of their own.

For Further Reflection

In what ways have you been made aware of the different kinds of literature (genres) in the Bible?

What sorts of questions might you ask of these different kinds, in order to understand them better?

Are some of these genres more relevant to some situations in life and less relevant to others—or can they all speak equally to all situations?

If their relevance differs, which situations is each genre most relevant to? How does this relate to what we know of their original contexts?

5
Who are Children?

'In any teaching there are two very important criteria to be met: the integrity of the subject, and the nature (needs, interest, stage of development, ability) of those we are teaching.'[16] In using the Bible with children, we have to ask not only, 'What is the Bible?' but, 'Who are the children we are teaching?' It seems to me that we need to be aware of a number of issues relating to the children we are working with, including their culture, their ways of learning, and their spiritual status and ways of development, so that we can better understand how to make our use of the Bible with them appropriate.

The Cultural Context of Children Today
1. Fragmentation of Community
Family life has been gradually taking a different shape over the past forty years, with a sharp increase in the number of divorces and the incidence of lone-parent households. There is also increasing fragmentation in the wider community. It is commonplace for a family to move several times, often to completely different parts of the country, in connection with a parent's work. Whereas fifty years ago, in rural areas and towns, families might have lived within a few streets of each other, the nuclear (rather than the extended) family is now the normal basic group. Moreover, as rural communities have died out and cities have decayed, there has been a gradual shift of the population to sprawling suburban areas, often 'commuter lands,' where even the neighbours are not known. In the cities and suburbs, with an increasingly multicultural and multifaith dimension, it has become more difficult for children of all cultures to find a community with which to identify.

2. Fragmentation of Beliefs
There has also been a fragmentation of the old belief-systems. The postmodern denial of the possibility of arriving at objective truth means that Christianity must rethink its apologetics, formerly so dependent on modern, rationalist, arguments. Meanwhile, the decline in church attendance among both adults and children means that we must recognize the fact that most of today's children and their parents have little or no understanding of Christian basics. So far as most children are concerned, it is not just that they do not know the *facts* of the Bible stories. It is that they have not been brought up in homes which even pretend to teach or practise Christian *values*.

---

16   Jean Holm, 'What Shall We Tell The Children?' *Theology* vol 76 (1973) pp 141–148, 147.

How Children Learn

It is a commonplace that 'to hear is to forget; to see is to remember; to do is to understand.' While traditional models of education have focussed on teacher-led lessons, the greatest insight of contemporary learning theories is that children (and adults) need to be actively engaged in their own learning. Moreover, while there has been an emphasis in the past on the cognitive (thinking) process in education, there is now increasing recognition that *all* faculties need to be engaged for the most fruitful learning. Small children, in particular, learn concretely using the five senses, but all of us have these capacities, which are especially underused in the evangelical (more word-based) tradition. There has also been some new valuing of the place of the emotions and intuition in the learning process. While there can be dangers in an ill-disciplined 'romanticism,' it seems to me right that some thought is now given to the more 'feminine' ways of knowing, as well as to the traditionally 'masculine' skills of logic and analysis. The educator Kieran Egan writes of the way in which the traditional focus on cognitive skills has denied a place to emotional understanding, and suggests that we need to recover the role of the imagination in teaching and learning.[17] Certainly, it seems to me more holistic to try to hold cognitive and affective meaning together. I think, again, of the Jewish, or Orthodox, rituals, so full of imagery, taste, colour, and sound, as well as the spoken word, which make some of our liturgies seem sterile—and not nearly so appealing to children.

Children also learn by doing. The truth of this has been recognized in much current children's group teaching material, in the place given to creative activities linked to the teaching theme. But I suggest that it might be possible to go further and apply 'doing' to Bible study itself. Much teaching material comes with a 'closed' message or moral included within it which leaders are expected to convey to the children as the 'point' of the lesson. Would it not be more fruitful, however, to build on the insight of educational theory that children retain more of what they do than of what they hear, by teaching them the skills to do Bible study and to begin to interpret for themselves?

Children's Faith

Are children part of the church or not? If they are, what level of spiritual understanding can we expect them to have, and in what ways can we expect them to be influenced by the Holy Spirit? All these questions deserve fuller treatment than I can give here, but it is perhaps helpful to raise awareness of them, because they all impinge on the issue of using the Bible with children.

---

17 *Teaching as Storytelling* (London: Routledge, 1988).

1. Children: In or Out of the Kingdom?

Is it appropriate to consider children 'saved,' or are they merely potential Christians? The answer to this question not only affects what we think we are doing when we teach children from the Bible (that is, discipling or evangelizing); it affects how we view children's capacity to take their part, along with adults, in the unfolding 'Big Story' of the people of God.

Little is said *directly* in the Bible about the issue, but the Old Testament seems to *assume* that children were included in the ritual life of the community, and male babies were circumcised as *the* sign of covenant acceptance. The New Testament records Jesus' teaching that 'the kingdom of heaven belongs to such as these' (Mt 19.14). Yet it is the norm for children to be marginalized in the life of the Christian community, and for them to be seen as somehow not fully part of the body.

John Inchley argues persuasively against seeing children as 'unsaved,' preferring to see them as 'in' the kingdom until such time as they have sufficient information and understanding to enable them to make a choice to opt 'in' or 'out.'[18] Francis Bridger suggests that while an adult-appropriate model of sin and accountability should not be applied to children, they are nevertheless capable of giving themselves to Christ within the limits of their own understanding.[19] My own experience is that I find evangelism and nurture merging together in my work with children, because I tend to think in terms of 'discipling' children—that is, trying to give them enough understanding about Jesus to enable them to choose to follow him with as much of themselves as they understand. My own preference is to treat children in the church as fully part of the body, at least until they are eleven or so. Until then they are, quite appropriately, likely to identify their faith with that of those in the communities to which they belong.

2. Faith Development

Allied to the question, 'Can children have faith?' is the question, 'If they can, what sort of faith is it reasonable to expect them to have?' Various theories of faith development have been put forward. There seems a consensus, though, that for children under the age of about five, 'faith' is experienced as trust (or lack of it) within the child's primary relationships. For children aged between about six and twelve, the faith of the child's affiliative group, or community, is the most significant for the child, and is what the child is likely to identify with.[20] Much children's group material for older primary children is very sensitive to the significance of the affiliative *peer group*, al-

---

18 John Inchley, *All About Children* (Eastbourne: Coverdale House, 1976) ch 1.
19 Francis Bridger, *Children Finding Faith* (London: Scripture Union, 1988) p 111.
20 See, for instance, the work of James Fowler and John Westerhoff, summarized in *How Faith Grows* (London: The National Society / Church House Publishing, 1991).

though I believe that we need to be much more alive to the significance of the *whole congregation* as an affiliative group for children.

3. Children and the Holy Spirit

The need for the interaction of Word and Spirit would hardly need comment, were it not that we are considering the question of *children* and the Bible. The role of the Spirit in guiding those who read, hear, or interpret the Word is rarely in dispute so far as adults are concerned, even in the least charismatic of circles. Where children are concerned, however, there is less assurance. This may be due, in part, to the general lack of confidence about children's status as 'believers.' I suspect, though, that it is also due to the plain lack of careful consideration which the whole subject of children and the Holy Spirit has received. In his book, *The Holy Spirit and Spiritual Gifts*, Max Turner argues that the New Testament evidences a 'one-stage' model of reception of the Spirit at the time of conversion-initiation.

> 'There is simply no clear exegetical evidence to suggest that Luke, Paul or John envisaged the possibility that there were in the post-Easter church two classes of Christians, distinguished by whether or not they had received the Pentecostal gift of the Spirit. That there could be any "believers"who lacked the new Christian "Spirit of prophecy" was strictly an exceptional and anomalous possibility (as Acts 8 indicates), because this gift (with the charismata it afforded), was at the heart of the new life of salvation, service and mission.'[21]

Of course, the 'one-stage' model of reception of the Spirit relies on the use of the concept of 'conversion-initiation' to denote a broad spectrum of experience. There would be much here to consider so far as children are concerned, especially in the light of faith-development theories. Nevertheless, I would suggest that, if individual children can meaningfully be considered 'believers,' within the limits of their faith-development stage, then we must expect, and teach, that the Spirit will guide them as they come to study the Bible. By the same token, I think we will need to be open to the possibility that, as we teach children to interpret, the truth into which the Spirit will lead them may sometimes be new to us.

For Further Reflection

Think of the children in your congregation and your local area. How would you characterize their context and experiences? Are there significant differences between those within and those outside the church?

What do you believe about children's place in the kingdom and relation to the Holy Spirit? Are your views shared by the congregation?

---

21 Max Turner, *The Holy Spirit and Spiritual Gifts* (Carlisle: Paternoster, 1996) p 159.

6
Bringing the Bible and Children Together

There are, then, two major practical implications for the work we do in using the Bible with children. Firstly, we need to attend more than we have done in the past to telling the 'big story' to children, by sign and word. My conviction about this is reinforced both by the fact that children learn and make meaning in a 'storied' way, and by the evidence all around us of the fragmented culture and desperate need for identity of today's children. Secondly, given the Bible's own witness to a variety of modes of nurturing people in the faith, we need to teach children to encounter the Bible in a way which consciously respects the diversity of the biblical material.

Communicating the 'Big Story'
1. The Context

The indications are that more and more children are failing to have their spiritual needs met in the home; comparatively few children are able to receive any Christian influence in the home or at school; and their natural affiliative groups are mostly non-Christian ones. These factors, together with the fact that the Bible tells the story of a *corporate* faith, combine to persuade me that the church now urgently needs to recognize its responsibility to be an alternative community for children (and their parents), offering Christian teaching in the context of loving relationships which maybe unavailable elsewhere. In recent years, Christian educators have been calling on the church to adopt this vision of itself, and to enact the vision in the Sunday services, as well as throughout the week. At the moment little has been done in practice. Most local churches, if they make concessions to the presence of children at all, tend to see the children's work as taking place in a separate group. So far as children in the congregation are concerned, it is preferred that, even if they are seen, they are not heard—at least not in any meaningful sense. John Westerhoff argues that 'the church teaches most significantly through nurture in a worshipping, witnessing community of faith.'[22] He adds that '(t)he church's educational problem rests not in its educational program, but in the paradigm or model which undergirds its educational ministry— the agreed upon frame of reference which guides its educational efforts.'[23] Arguing for an essentially *relational* model of Christian education, he stresses that the first and most fundamental form of learning is by experience—after

---

22   J Westerhoff, *Will Our Children Have Faith?* (New York: Harper Collins, 1976) p 4.
23   *ibid* p 6.

which comes imaging (through the use of stories), and then conceptual learning. 'But first comes experience.'[24]

This insistence on learning in the faith community is reflective of the way in which the Jewish community taught, and teaches, its children. Hans-Rudi Weber speaks of the Jewish home as a 'continuous, theocentric educational institution.'[25] In the Gentile community, however, where comparatively few of today's parents, let alone the children, have had much exposure to the Christian tradition, an alternative 'family' is needed. In considering the question of what the church should teach its children, Jean Holm suggests that, while adults and adolescents need to be taught, perhaps the greatest need for children is to be shown that they *belong*.[26]

Not only can the all-age community provide an affiliative group for children: the relationships among its members, particularly in relation to the children, can model the kind of relationships God wants us to have with him and with each other. To children from abusive or unloving homes, no amount of word-based teaching will communicate the nature of the love of God for us, or the love we should have for others. Where children's 'experiencing' stage of faith has provided inadequate opportunities for understanding what love 'looks like,' there is a need for the church to offer the chance of 're-experiencing.' My contention is not that there is no need for age-related group work for children. The smaller, children-only group can provide a level and quantity of focussed teaching, activity and play which, though stimulating for children, would be inappropriate in an all-age context. My point is that, if we want to teach a biblical faith to our children, we must put the words of the Bible into action, and allow children, with us, to experience what it means to belong to a worshipping, witnessing community. If we fail to do this, our use of the Bible with children will be less than holistic.

2. The Content

Practical ways of enacting the 'big story' within the whole congregation include dramas, or voice-dramas, in which everyone has a small part (perhaps a few 'chorus' lines to chant or shout) and musicals (such as those by Roger Jones) which can incorporate a large cast. Christmas nativities, or simple 'passion plays,' are good ways to include almost everyone. Worship and celebration events enacting all or part of our 'story' need not take place in the church building. Last Hallowe'en we held a 'Light Party' for children and parents in the village hall, with games, food, and a simple act of worship round a candle symbolizing Jesus, the light of the world. Many congregations now enjoy Passover meals, with appropriate food and liturgy. Harvest

---

24   *ibid* p 63.
25   H-R Weber, *Jesus and the Children* (Geneva: World Council of Churches, 1979) p 40.
26   Jean Holm, 'What Shall We Tell The Children?' *Theology* vol LXXVI, no 633 March 1973, p 147.

thanksgiving suppers, too, can provide an excellent opportunity not just to share a meal but to celebrate all that God has done in our lives. My children's group hopes to make a church 'family tree,' with names and photographs of every adult and child in the congregation, to be linked in with the biblical 'family tree,' going back through Jesus to Abraham.

In the separate children's group one Sunday, we spent the session thinking about the overall story of the Bible, and then made 'evangelism bracelets,' to help us tell the story to others. Coloured beads were threaded on to gold elastic: white for God's good creation; black for the sin which spoiled it (check that this will not be racially offensive); red for the blood of Jesus; white for the fresh start he wants to give us; green for the new life of the Spirit in us; gold for the hope of heaven. The gold elastic signified the fact that Jesus 'ties us in' to himself and holds us.

Another idea for illustrating the 'Big Story' is a Bible 'time-line' drawn on a long piece of wallpaper, tacked on to the walls and left in place for several terms. The basic Bible events, with dates, are filled in, and as the group studies different texts over the weeks, illustrations are added to the time-line at the appropriate places.

In thinking about how to teach and illustrate the 'Big Story' in their own congregations and children's groups, leaders might find it helpful, as I have done, to 'brainstorm' with others. It is amazing how, over coffee and cake round the fire, creative ideas can emerge, and the gifts of each one combine to make a really exciting whole.

Teaching Children to Interpret

Seeing the Bible as presenting the unfolding story of the people of God, in which the community both acts in and records the drama, is a good way of opening the text up to interpretation and application with children.

The first task for teachers is to understand what level of Bible study is appropriate for the different age ranges. In his helpful and practical book on Bible study with children, Terry Clutterham points out that whereas pre-school children value stories but need concrete images, five- to seven-year-olds still enjoy stories but are able to start to think about the 'hidden' issues of themes, motives, and intrigues. Eight- to ten-year-olds will also enjoy stories, though in a less 'enchanted' way, and will have an increasing grasp of chronology and geography, so that they can begin to ask 'historical' questions of the text. Children aged eleven plus will be increasingly able to have a grasp of God's plan for the world and our part in it.[27]

R and G Gobbel suggest that, from the age of about six, children can be introduced to some of the different literary forms in the Bible, and assisted

---

27 T Clutterham, *The Adventure Begins* (Milton Keynes: Scripture Union, 1996) pp 132, 133.

to distinguish between them.[28] Stories, poetry, and letters can be identified, and the children can be helped to begin to ask appropriate questions of each type of material. So, for instance, of the narratives, children can learn to ask 'Was this a story which someone (for example Jesus) told, or does it record a real event?'; 'When and where were the events happening?'; 'What was happening elsewhere in the world at that time?'; 'What were people's everyday lives like then?'; 'Are there any particular words which need explanation?'(for instance, 'centurion,' 'talents,' 'Samaritan'). Of poetic material, such as the psalms, it can be appropriate to ask 'What was the writer feeling?'; 'What did he/she want to express?'; 'What are some of the key images/pictures being used?'; 'Why?'; 'How would I express the same feelings?' (Then try—perhaps with some suitable music playing in the background, and the use of paints, dance, or mime, as well as words). Where letters are concerned, questions need to be asked about the situations of both the senders and the receivers. It is always interesting to try to do the 'detective' work of piecing together the issues which brought about the letter in the first place, and it can be an interesting exercise for children to try to formulate their own letter dealing with the situation, or the letter which brought about the biblical letter in reply. Older children can be introduced to the more challenging prophetic material, and to some of the dreams. Of prophecy, it would be appropriate to ask 'When was the prophet speaking?'; 'What was the situation which was being addressed?'; 'Why?'; 'What might the prophet want to challenge today?'; 'What could we do about it?' Of dreams, questions could be asked about the significant imagery, and what it might mean, as well as about the historical context of the 'dreamer.'

It will be important to allow children time to 'play' with the text, so that their thoughts and questions can surface. We also need to remember to frame our questions of the children in 'open' ways, rather than in 'closed' ways which neatly suggest our own answers. We must, I think, expect that the children will have some new insights to share with us. Just as the writers of the epistles did their theology 'on the hoof,' dealing constantly with unprecedented situations, so children, whose world is sometimes so different from our own, must be given scope to find their own appropriate applications.

On a practical note, I think it is almost essential for each child to have access to a suitable Bible for the purposes of study. There are various appropriate versions, including the NIV and the Good News Bible, although neither of these is gender-inclusive.[29] Our group has decided to use the New Century Version, which does use inclusive language, and which has both a children's version (with pictures and clear print) for children aged up to,

---

28 R and G Gobbel, *The Bible: A Child's Playground* (London: SCM, 1986) pp 119–122.
29 On the general question of versions, see R T France *Translating the Bible: choosing and using an English version* (Grove Biblical booklet B 3).

say, eleven or twelve, and a youth version, with comments, for teenagers. There are on the market various sets of children's and young people's Bible-reading notes, and church groups might like to think about investing in a regular copy for each child, at least for an initial period, in order to encourage children to read and study the Bible for themselves at home.

7

Conclusion

My impression is that, in practice, in the church today, there is a lack of confidence about teaching the value of regular, thoughtful, Bible study. Little enough is done to encourage *adults* to read the Bible intelligently, so it is hardly surprising that the subject of *children's* Bible study has not merited much serious consideration. Too often, we want to ask the 'how' questions without first asking the 'why' questions, and in consequence little is done to examine the principles underlying our use of the Bible in children's ministry. I have tried here to begin to explore the issues. Possibly, more thought could be given to the question of a children's hermeneutic. But already, it seems to me, we have available sufficient material on biblical interpretation and children's learning issues to make good teaching of interpretational skills to children long overdue. By failing to teach children to study the Bible for themselves, or to study it with them, we are all being left the poorer. An old rabbinical dictum says: 'Don't limit children to your own learning, for they were born in another time.' Just as children can be enriched by their study of the Bible, so can we be. As children need our experience and wisdom as we tell them the old truths, so we need theirs as they tell us the new truths. If we only give children the results of our own (often half-hearted) Bible study, we shall limit them to our own learning. If we, rather, give them the skills to explore the Bible for themselves, listen respectfully to their insights, and encourage them to find practical applications, then we can begin to discover *together* what it means to belong to Jesus Christ, to share his life, and to participate in the ongoing story of his grace and love.

8
Some Helpful Books

The Bible and Bible Study

W Brueggemann, *The Creative Word* (Philadelphia: Fortress, 1988)—thought-provoking, though densely written, on the clues in the OT to teaching the faith.

G Fee and D Stuart, *How to Read the Bible for All its Worth* (London: Scripture Union, 1994)—helpful, straightforward introduction to beginning Bible study.

J Goldingay, *Models for Scripture* (Grand Rapids: Eerdmans, 1994)—more academic but very readable discussion of models for the way in which we understand the Bible.

D McCartney and C Clayton, *Let the Reader Understand* (Wheaton: Bridgepoint, 1994)—lively and scholarly introduction to Bible study.

W Wink, *Transforming Bible Study* (Abingdon: Nashville, 1989)—stimulating and original approach to group Bible study, using 'left- and right-brain' theory.

N T Wright, *The New Testament and the People of God* (London: SPCK, 1992)—rich and challenging first volume of series on Christian origins.

Children's Ministry

J Cray, *Seen and Heard* (Crowborough: Monarch, 1995)—helpful resource material on ways of including children in church life.

P Frank, *Leading Children* (Nottingham: St John's Extension Studies, 1998)—creative and practical material for children's leaders on understanding today's children, and introducing them to the Christian faith.

P Graystone, *Help! There's a Child in My Church* (London: Scripture Union, 1989)—readable and sensitive introduction to children and church.

P Graystone and E Turner, *A Church for All Ages* (London: Scripture Union, 1993)—helpful introduction to all-age worship.

C and J Leach, *And For Your Children* (Crowborough: Monarch, 1994)—practical discussion of children and the Holy Spirit.

D Ng and E Thomas, *Children in the Worshipping Community* (Atlanta: John Knox, 1981)—American experience of church for all ages.

Children and the Bible

T Clutterham, *The Adventure Begins* (Milton Keynes: Scripture Union, 1996)—good practical handbook on Bible study with children and young people.

D Furnish, *Experiencing the Bible With Children* (Nashville: Abingdon, 1990)—innovative approach, drawing on the use of story, drama and dance.

R and G Gobbel, *The Bible: A Child's Playground* (London: SCM, 1986)—thought-provoking ideas on children's capacity to interpret.

P Van Ness, *Transforming Bible Study With Children* (Nashville: Abingdon, 1991)—development of W Wink's work on inductive Bible study.

R Willoughby, *Children's Guide to the Bible* (Milton Keynes: Scripture Union, 1998)—attractive and informative guide for children—and their parents and leaders.